THE DAY THE FAT LADY SINGS

A Biblical Study on End Time Events

By "Papa Joe" De Clemente

THE DAY THE FAT LADY SINGS

Copyright June 2023

THE DAY THE FAT LADY SINGS

Table of Contents

THE DAY THE FAT LADY SINGS

FOREWORD

Before I start this adventure in writing about the "End Times", I would like to take this opportunity to thank my son, Joseph III, who gave me the idea and inspiration to go ahead with this project. I would also like to take this time to clarify a couple of things: This paper was written to provide one particular point of view of the end time events. I am in no way stating that this view is absolutely correct and is free from errors. I am not. I believe that I am an "Average Joe" with a view of eschatology that should be addressed, written down and explained.

If the future unfolds in the manner that is presented within the next pages, it is not because I feel that I had some super revelation. It is only the things that I see coming to pass as I have read the Holy Scriptures.

I would also like to make it clear that my views have not come about because of any books that I have read. The books that I have read about end times have always leaned toward the Pre-Tribulation Rapture of the Church.

THE DAY THE FAT LADY SINGS

I would like to state it here and now, so that it not be misunderstood, that I prefer to believe in the Pre-Tribulation Rapture of the Church rather than any other points of view however, that is not what I see when I read the Scriptures.

If all else fails, I hope that the reader finds this paper interesting and that in some way he or she may be drawn closer to the Lord Jesus, who shall be forever praised.

THE DAY THE FAT LADY SINGS

DEFINITIONS

At this time, I believe that it would be appropriate to elaborate on the some of the words used and what is the meaning of each. Again, may I state, that I have not gone back into the Hebrew or the Greek to support the position that I am taking here. It is merely a matter of how the words and scripture have impressed me and what I believe to be their intent.

1. Christian: A person, who not only believes that Jesus is God the Son and has died for their sins, but has accepted Jesus as their personal Savior. Believing that apart from His Sacrifice on the Cross, and His Blood Atonement (Saving Grace), there is no hope of salvation from their sins.

2. The Church: It is not a building. It is the body of believers who have accepted Jesus as Lord and Savior. Those who are "Born Again" in Christ per John 3:3. You have accepted Jesus' sacrifice on the Cross and only His shed Blood pays for all sins and we are therefore righteous because of what He did at Calvary.

THE DAY THE FAT LADY SINGS

It is NOT because of any good works that we think we have done. It is a Gift of God per the scriptures:

Ephesians 2:8-9.

[8] *For it is by grace you have been saved, through faith—and this is not from yourselves, it is the gift of God—* [9] *not by works, so that no one can boast*

3. Rapture: An event where Jesus sends His angels to collect the real Christians (or Believers);
   1st) those who have died and;
   2nd) those who are still alive.

4. Tribulation: It is a period in time, when there will be PEACE for 3½ years and then CHAOS & CALAMITY for 3½ years under the ruling of the "ANTICHRIST". The second 3½ years is also known as the Time of Jacob's Trouble, where the Antichrist will go after the Jewish believers (144 Thousand).

5. Distress: The "Great Distress of those days" as spoken of in Matthew 24:29, refers to the Tribulation Period (possibly all 7 years, but definitely the second 3½ years).

6. God's Wrath: Refers to "GOD's WRATH" on mankind. It should not be confused with man's wrath upon other humans, such as the Antichrist's actions against those who are believers. It is an extreme action that God takes upon mankind to be used as a punishment.

A good example is the plagues against pharaoh & Egypt in Exodus. It should not be confused with "minor" weather changes or earthquakes, which may be used to announce the coming of some event that God has planned.

THE DAY THE FAT LADY SINGS

BASIS OF BELIEF

Although some may say that the book of Revelation is a complex book containing a lot of figurative speech and writings, I have approached this book on the basis that our God is a God of order and not disorder. Therefore, my Scripture approach is that the end time events will flow in an orderly pattern, which can easily be linked to the Gospels and other Old and New Testament passages. In addition, I believe that Matthew 24 is a summary of the events detailed in Revelation and that the events in Revelation will run somewhat parallel to what happened to the Israelites of old, namely Moses and Aaron, in regard to the "Promise Land". Prior to his leaving for the promise land, the world, as he knew it, namely Egypt, had to undergo a number of plagues generated by God, while keeping the Israelites safe, through the shed blood of the lambs. The plagues came, but the Israelites were kept safe through their faith and obedience.

Keeping this in mind, let's move onto the "End Time" events.

THE DAY THE FAT LADY SINGS

THE BOOK OF MATTHEW

When asked about the destruction of the Temple and the end times, Jesus replied to His disciple, "Watch out that no one deceives you. For many will come…." and He continues the description throughout the rest of the gospel of Matthew, Chapter 24. He did not leave them without any clues or signs of the times. He gave them a real response with some signs that they were to look for. If we read Matthew 24, we can list them in the order that Jesus spoke of them. There will be:

1. Deceivers claiming to be Him
2. Wars and Rumors of wars (nation against nation)
3. Famines
4. Earthquakes
5. Persecution
6. Turning away from the Faith
7. Betrayers & Haters
8. Increase of Wickedness & Coldness in people's heart (Love will grow cold)
9. Gospel will preached to the whole world
10. Then the END WILL COME

These were some of the key signs that Jesus' followers were to look for.

THE DAY THE FAT LADY SINGS

However Jesus continues His elaboration with a couple of additional major signs that he adds at the end:

11. When you see the Abomination that causes Desolations in the Holy Place
12. Then He talks about them looking for the Christ in the fields (watch out for this)
13. Great signs being done to deceive even the elect, if it were possible
14. Where there is a Carcass, there the Vultures will gather
15. IMMEDIATELY after the Great Distress of those days
16. The Sun will Darken
17. The Stars will fall
18. The Heavenly Bodies will be shaken
19. THEN the Sign of the Son of Man will appear in the Sky and all the nations will mourn.
20. They will see the Son of Man coming on clouds to gather His elect from the four winds.

THE DAY THE FAT LADY SINGS

Then Jesus told them to watch and look for the signs as one would look at a Fig Tree to see when it will give its fruit. He did state, in verse 36 of Matthew 24, "no one will know the day or hour", when the end shall come, HOWEVER, Jesus does say that "as it was in the days of NOAH, so it will be at the coming of the Son of Man".

In other words, BE PREPARED and WATCH FOR THE SIGNS. In this manner, you'll know when things are going to unfold before you. The signs will help us be prepared. They can act as a double check for us to keep true to the faith.

THE DAY THE FAT LADY SINGS

THE BOOK OF MARK

Does the Book of Mark read in the same fashion as Matthew?? Let's look at Mark 13:4 thru 13:37 and summarize it. It states:

1. Deceivers claiming to be Him
2. Wars and Rumors of wars (nation against nation)
3. Earthquakes
4. Famines
5. **"These are the beginning of birth pains" (Mark 13:8)**
6. Persecution
7. You will stand before……..as my witnesses
8. Family betrayals over the Gospel's sake
9. **Then the END WILL COME (Mark 13:13)**
10. Abomination that causes desolation
11. **Warning: It will be dreadful for pregnant women**
12. Great Distress of those days unequaled from the beginning
13. False Christ to appear
14. Miracles to deceive the Elect
15. The Sun and Moon will darken
16. The Stars will fall
17. The Heavenly bodies will be shaken
18. They will see the coming of the Son of Man (Mark 13:26)

THE DAY THE FAT LADY SINGS

19. He will send his angels out to gather
the Elect (Mark 13:37)

When we chart Matthew and Mark, we can now see if there is any pattern in the signs detailed in each Gospel.

EVENT	Matthew	Mark		
	In order of occurrence			
Deceivers claiming to be Him	1	1		
Wars and Rumors of Wars	2	2		
Famine	3	4		
Earthquakes	4	3		
Persecution	5	5		
Turning away from the Faith	6			
Betrayers & Haters	7	6		
Increase in Wickedness	8			
Gospel preached throughout the World	9			
Abomination		7		
Great Distress		8		
False Christ		9		
False Miracles		10		
Sun Darken		11		
Heavenly Bodies Fall		12		
Sign in the sky of the coming of the Son of God		13		
Angels will gather the elect		14		

THE DAY THE FAT LADY SINGS

THE BOOK OF LUKE

How does the Book of Luke read?? Is it similar to Matthew and Mark? Let's look at Luke 21:7 thru 21:36. It states:

1. Deceivers claiming to be Him
2. Wars and Rumors of wars (nation against nation)
3. Earthquakes
4. Famines
5. Persecution
6. You will be my Witnesses
7. Betrayers & Haters
8. See Jerusalem surrounded by the Armies, then Desolation is near
9. **Warning: It will be dreadful for pregnant women**
10. Jerusalem will be trampled by the Gentiles
11. The Sun and Moon will darken
12. The Stars will fall
13. The Heavenly bodies will be shaken
14. They will see the coming of the Son of Man (Luke 21:27)
15. Stand up and Lift your heads, because your Redemption is near (Luke 21:28)

THE DAY THE FAT LADY SINGS

At this point, I would ask you to briefly look at the pattern in the three (3) Gospels and how they sum up the end times and get your first glimpse at what may happen. Remember, the signs were given, by Jesus, directly as He told them to his disciples. They are His words, not mine. Let's see if the same pattern continues:

EVENT	Matthew	Mark	Luke
	In order of occurrence		
Deceivers claiming to be Him	1	1	1
Wars and Rumors of Wars	2	2	2
Famine	3	4	4
Earthquakes	4	3	3
Persecution	5	5	5
Turning away from the Faith	6		
Betrayers & Haters	7	6	6
Increase in Wickedness	8		
Gospel preached throughout the World	9		
Abomination		7	7
Great Distress		8	
False Christ		9	
False Miracles		10	
Sun Darken		11	8
Heavenly Bodies Fall		12	9
Sign in the sky of the coming of the Son of God		13	10
Angels will gather the elect		14	11

So far we seem to be developing a pattern. Does the book of Thessalonians fit the pattern? Let's see.

THE DAY THE FAT LADY SINGS

1 THESSALONIANS

Chapter 4:13 – 17

13 Brothers, we do not want you to be ignorant about those who fall asleep, or to grieve like the rest of men, who have no hope.

14 We believe that Jesus died and rose again and so we believe that God will bring with Jesus those who have fallen asleep in him.

15 According to the Lord's own word, we tell you that we who are still alive, who are left till the coming of the Lord, will certainly not precede those who have fallen asleep.

16 For the Lord himself, will come down from heaven, with a loud command, with the voice of the archangel and with the trumpet call *(1 Corinthians 15:52 states "the sound of the LAST trumpet")* **of God, and the dead in Christ will rise first.**

17 After that, we who are still alive and are left will be caught up together with them *(or the RAPTURE of the CHURCH)* in the clouds to meet the Lord in the air. And so we will be with the Lord forever.

THE DAY THE FAT LADY SINGS

Chapter 5:1 - 9

1 Now, brothers, about times and dates we do not need to write to you,

2 for you know very well that the day of the Lord will come like a thief in the night.

3 While people are saying, "Peace and safety," destruction will come on them suddenly, as labor pains on a pregnant woman, and they will not escape.

4 But you, brothers, are not in darkness so that this day should surprise you like a thief.

5 You are all sons of the light and sons of the day. We do not belong to the night or to the darkness.

6 So then, let us not be like others, who are asleep, but let us be alert and self-controlled.

7 For those who sleep, sleep at night, and those who get drunk, get drunk at night.

8 But since we belong to the day, let us be self-controlled, putting on faith and love as a breastplate, and the hope of salvation as a helmet.

9 For God did not appoint us to suffer wrath _(GOD's WRATH)_ **but to receive salvation through our Lord Jesus Christ.**

THE DAY THE FAT LADY SINGS

Based upon the above, we may state that:

1. The Lord's Archangel will sound the Trumpet Call to announce the Lord's Grand Intervention on mankind.
2. The Rapture of the Church will take place
3. While people are proclaiming "Peace and safety", trying to make heads or tails of the situation, destruction will come upon them suddenly. This has to be the Lord's Wrath upon the unbelievers, after the believers have been removed.

   NOTES:
   a) Believers should NOT be in darkness about this, and;
   b) The Believers will NOT suffer from GOD's WRATH.

So to answer our question; "Does the Book of First Thessalonians fit the pattern?"

I would say "YES, IT DOES"

Now let's get on to the Book of Revelation where the real meat is.

THE DAY THE FAT LADY SINGS

THE BOOK OF REVELATION

Now comes the last part. Let's see if we put the Book of Revelation into a perspective, which will be easily understood. Remember, Jesus' recorded words in the Gospels should never be contradicted. The Lord doesn't say one thing today and something entirely different tomorrow. He is the same yesterday, today and tomorrow. Whatever Jesus spoke about in the Gospels should align itself to some occurrence in Revelation. However, we may consider the verses spoken in the Gospels to be summaries of what Revelation is all about. The Gospels provided the summary and Revelation provides the details.

Please note that the following passages in Revelation may occur over the following periods of time, however we really do not know:

Chapters 4 through 6 occur over some unknown period of time (possibly 50 years).
Chapters 7 through 10 occur over some 10 to 20 years (guesstimate).
Chapter 11, verses 1 through 14 occurs for a period of 3½ years (42 months).
Chapter 11:15 through Chapter 14: 13 occurs over about another 3½ years.
Chapter 14:14 through Chapter 19 may take a very short period of time (½ to 2 years)

THE DAY THE FAT LADY SINGS

All we really have to do is READ, WATCH, and BE ALERT as to what the Lord has planned before us. So let's start with Chapter 1.

CHAPTER 1

The Apostle John opens up with a greeting and a doxology. He then goes on to tell us what happened to him when he was on the island of Patmos (v 9). On the Lord's Day, he had a vision and saw the Lord Jesus, the Alpha and Omega. He then was told to write down what will happen, in regard to the seven churches.

Some say that the seven churches represent the churches through the ages, while others believe that they are the churches that existed at the time of John's writing. I tend to go along with the later, since the characteristics of the churches could even represent seven types of churches that exist today:

THE DAY THE FAT LADY SINGS

CHAPTER 2 and 3

The characteristics of the seven churches:

#1 Ephesus lost its First Love,

#2 Smyrna gave up when they were persecuted

#3 Pergamum held to the teaching of Balaam

#4 Thyatira was misled into Sexual Immorality

#5 Sardis was a Dead Church

#6 Philadelphia was a Church of Liars

#7 Laodicea was Lukewarm

Whichever position you may take on the above, the key point here is that we should make sure that we are not a member of one of those churches. Does our life display a characteristic of one of those churches? If so, then we should make every effort to repent and ask the Lord to change us.

THE DAY THE FAT LADY SINGS

CHAPTER 4

The scripture states that; "After this I looked and there before me was a door standing open in Heaven. And the voice I had first heard in heaven speaking to me like a trumpet said, 'Come up here and I will show you what must take place after this.'"

This passage also lends itself to the position that the seven churches were real churches at that time, but most important here is that the voice that called out stated that John would see what must take place after the vision he had (aka: the future, time unknown).

Then the four (4) creatures in Heaven gave God the Glory and worshipped Him.

CHAPTER 5

"Then I saw in the right hand of Him who sat on the Throne a scroll with writing on both sides and sealed with seven (7) seals". "Who is worthy to break the seals…?" Only one person was worthy to break the seals and that was the "Root of Jesse", "The Lion of Judah", JESUS, he was worthy. So they worshipped and Praised Him who was worthy to break the seven (7) seals and the four creatures said "Amen" and the elders fell down and worshipped".

THE DAY THE FAT LADY SINGS

Okay, we are all excited about what is happening, and we want to know what will take place next. Jesus, the Lamb of God starts to open or break the seals and one (1) of the four living creatures says "Come" and there before me (John speaking) was what??

The words "before me" could mean that John was looking into the future at this point. When or what time period is unknown, but we know what he sees, because he wrote it down. With each seal being broke, he sees the following:

#1 - White Horse with a Rider or Conqueror on a Conquest.

#2 – Fiery Red Horse with a Rider to take Peace from the earth

.

#3 – Black Horse with a Rider with a Pair of Scales.

#4 – Pale Horse with a Rider named Death.

#5 – He saw the souls of those who had be slain because of the Word of God and the Testimony that they maintained.

THE DAY THE FAT LADY SINGS

#6 – A Great Earthquake occurred and the Moon turned blood red, stars fell and the earth was shaken, quite bad. The people of the earth hid themselves from the Lord in fear.

At this point the seventh (#7) seal is not opened yet, but it will be soon. So let's ask ourselves, what are the seals? Are they God's wrath on mankind or is it the consequence of man's wrath on himself. Maybe they are just the signs of things to happen before something big occurs.

THE DAY THE FAT LADY SINGS

Have we seen these signs before?? Do they match those stated in the Gospels above?? Let's go back to our Chart:

EVENT	Matthew	Mark	Luke	Revelation
	In order of occurrence			(SEAL #)
Deceivers claiming to be Him	1	1	1	
Wars and Rumors of Wars	2	2	2	# 2 (6:3)
Famine	3	4	4	# 3, (6"5) # 4 (6: 7)
Earthquakes	4	3	3	
Persecution	5	5	5	# 5 (6:9)
Turning away from the Faith	6			
Betrayers & Haters	7	6	6	
Increase in Wickedness	8			
Gospel preached throughout the World	9			
Abomination		7	7	
Great Distress		8		
False Christ		9		
False Miracles		10		
Sun Darken		11	8	
Heavenly Bodies Fall		12	9	# 6 (6:12)
Sign in the sky of the coming of the Son of God		13	10	
Angels will gather the elect		14	11	

THE DAY THE FAT LADY SINGS

CHAPTER 7

The scripture states that after this, in the future after the above signs, John saw four angels who had power to hurt the land and the people were told to wait until the servants of God were sealed, the 144,000 from the tribes of Israel. The numbers and the tribes are stated in verses 5 through 8.

After this, again in the future still, praise was given to the Lord and one of the angels asked about the people who were in white robes. The answer was simple. It was they who have come out of the great tribulation. So we know that those who are slain come after the sealing of the 144,000 Jews.

THE DAY THE FAT LADY SINGS

CHAPTER 8

In the chapter 8, the Seventh Seal is opened and another angel takes the censer filled with fire and hurls it down to earth where an earthquake happens and peals of lightning start. The Seven Trumpets also begin to sound.

Trumpet #1 – Hail and Fire destroy trees and grass

Trumpet #2 – A huge mountain is thrown into the sea destroying some sea life.

Trumpet #3 – A great Star falls into the rivers and the waters become bitter.

Trumpet #4 – The Sun, Moon and Stars are struck.

CHAPTER 9

Trumpet #5 – A Star fell and Locust came forth to harm unsaved people.

Trumpet #6 – A great wind unleashed the River Euphrates, mounted troops (2 hundred million) came to kill mankind. More plagues started killing mankind.

THE DAY THE FAT LADY SINGS

CHAPTER 10

Chapter 10 describes John's vision of an angel with a little scroll. The voice of Seven (7) Thunders was heard, but John was not permitted to write down what they said. It was supposed to be sealed up as a mystery.

This gives us a brief glimpse of something that happens which will remain unknown to us for now.

THE DAY THE FAT LADY SINGS

CHAPTER 11

In chapter 11, we see the Holy City is trampled down for 42 months (3 ½ years). This is the "Abomination" that causes desolation spoken about in the Gospels and the Old Testament. Then the Lord will have two (2) witnesses who will testify for 1,260 days, which is also 42 months. Their likeness will be that of Moses and Aaron preaching to the Israelites and to Pharaoh in Exodus, chapter 7. However, these two (2) witnesses will be slain after the 42 months. After 3 ½ days, the breath of life from God (v 11) will enter them, they will be taken up to heaven and terror will strike those who see them.

After this the Seventh Angel will sound its trumpet (v 15), those in heaven praised the Lord and the final episode will begin.

REMEMBER *1 Thessalonians 4?*

16 For the Lord himself, will come down from heaven, with a loud command, with the voice *of* **the archangel and with the trumpet call** *(some versions state "the sound of the last trumpet")* **of God, and the dead in Christ will rise first.**

THE DAY THE FAT LADY SINGS

I believe that this seventh trumpet call is also the last trumpet call stated in 1 Thessalonians. So God begins the "Grand Finale" of his plan for us humans. The following chapters (11 through 14) in Revelation may actually happen quite rapidly and close to each other.

CHAPTER 12

In Chapter 12, two (2) signs appear in heaven. The first being the woman clothed with the sun (probably Israel) and the 2nd being the Red Dragon (or Satan) who goes after the woman. She hides for 1,260 days (or 3 ½ years). Henceforth, the Dragon goes after her offspring.

Question: When does this happen?? Does this happen during the first 3 ½ years or the second 3 ½ years?

Answer: Since the first 3 ½ years is supposed to be peaceful and the witnesses are not killed until the first 3 ½ years are done, it has to be in the second 3 ½ years. And, since it is Israel (the natural branches of the vine) which is in danger, it could be called the "Time of Jacob's Trouble". Henceforth, the Time of Jacob's Trouble is during the second part of the Great Tribulation, but not necessarily the same time when God pours out His wrath upon mankind.

THE DAY THE FAT LADY SINGS

CHAPTER 13

Then he, who comes out of the Earth, is obviously the Antichrist. He is from Earth and he is the Beast. He is fatally wounded and then recovers. He utters blasphemies and is given authority to war against the "SAINTS" and conquer them. Guess what guys? We believers are still here and the Beast is after us. We are some of the offspring (or fruits and braches) of the vine, Israel, spoken about in Chapter 12. All the inhabitants of the earth will worship the Beast, except those whose names are written in the book belonging to the Lamb, aka: the Believers (verse 8). "THIS CALL FOR PATIENT ENDURANCE AND FAITHFULNESS ON THE PART OF THE SAINTS" (verse 10b). WHY?? Because, we will NOT be exempt from the persecution from the Beast. So Brothers and Sisters, hold onto your hats and stay firm in the faith.

Then John sees another beast coming forth from the earth; the Anti-Christ's assistant, I presume. He follows the orders of the first Beast and he orders the inhabitants to set up an IMAGE of the BEAST. He also gives the IMAGE life so that it could speak and kill those who did not worship the first beast.

THE DAY THE FAT LADY SINGS

The IMAGE forces everyone to receive a MARK on the right hand or forehead, so that could buy and sell. However, only true believers will not receive this mark.

What is the IMAGE of the Beast?

It may very well be an Artificial Intelligence (AI) Mainframe Computer, which holds all of the necessary information on everyone in the world. Is this possible? Yes! We now live in a world where this is very possible. This AI computer could be programmed to reflect exactly what the Beast wants and demands. All must bow down and worship him in order to buy or sell (survive). Get the Mark and you will live. Otherwise you die by starvation.

How did he give it life?? He probably just turned the main power switch "ON" and programmed it.

What is the MARK of the Beast?

Maybe it's a transponder that is implanted under the skin? All this is possible and actually feasible today.

But again, this is only a guess on my part.

THE DAY THE FAT LADY SINGS

CHAPTER 14

"Then I looked and there before me..." (Meaning "in the future"), verses 1 through 5 show the 144,000 Jews who remained pure and did not worship the beast. They sang a new song before the throne, the four living creatures and the Elders. Sounds like they will in Heaven shortly.

The John saw three angels:

Angel #1 said, "Fear God and give Him Glory"

Angel #2 said, "Fallen is Babylon the Great"

Angel #3 gives warning about the Beast and the Mark. Anyone receiving the Mark will drink of the wine of God's fury, or His Wrath, which is still yet to come.

In verse 14 of Chapter 14, we see God sending out His angels to, "reap, because the time to reap has come". This sounds like the rapture spoken about in Matthew 24:20, Mark 13:16 and Luke 21:14. And, it is also the vision that is spoken about in 1 Thessalonians 4:17 after the sound of the 7th Trumpet spoken about in Revelation 11:15.

THE DAY THE FAT LADY SINGS

Then another angel comes out to gather those who will suffer from God's Wrath (v 19). So God's Wrath is finally poured out.

CHAPTER 15

The scripture states that seven angels will come out and give the earth seven plagues from God. The plagues are contained within the bowls. These are God's Bowls of Wrath. The angels are prepared and waiting for God's command to proceed. Sounds like the Egypt scene is about ready to happen all over again.

THE DAY THE FAT LADY SINGS

CHAPTER 16

Stating in chapter 16, we now see the Bowls of God's Wrath poured out onto mankind:

Bowl #1 - Ugly Sores break out on those who have the mark of the beast.

Bowl #2 – The Sea turns into blood

Bowl #3 – The Rivers and the Spring Water turns into blood

Bowl #4 – The Sun scorches the people with fire

So what do the people do?? How stupid, they curse God!!! Egypt "Deja-vu".

Bowl #5 – God's Wrath is poured out onto the beast, and his kingdom plunges into darkness.

Bowl #6 – The great river Euphrates dries up to leave a path for the kings of the east.

At this point, the demons are let loose (vs 14) to stir up the kings of the world to get them ready for the battle of Armageddon.

THE DAY THE FAT LADY SINGS

Bowl #7 – More of God's Wrath is poured out and a great earthquake occurs, bigger than the earlier ones and the great city splits into three parts. From the sky, huge hailstones, about 100 pounds each, fall on man.

So what do the people do? Being really stupid, they curse God again! Doesn't man ever learn from his actions?

Just a small note here. Please notice that the Bowls of God's Wrath happen after the angels are sent out to collect the elect from the four winds of the earth as described in Revelation 14:14. This sounds like the post tribulation rapture of the church to me!!

THE DAY THE FAT LADY SINGS

CHAPTER 17

Chapter 17 describes the woman (a prostitute) who sits and commits adultery with those on earth. On her forehead was written:

Mystery
Babylon the Great
The Mother of Prostitutes
And of the abominations of the earth

She is drunk with the blood of the saints, but soon she will meet her demise (See Chapter 18), because in chapter 17, God is getting ready for her.

CHAPTER 18

The Fall of Babylon, consumed with fire because the Lord has judged her. Everyone will mourn at her. She was great, but now she is gone. Not much can be explained except what is seen through John's eyes here.

CHAPTER 19

HALLELJAH!!!   After this, John sees a multitude in heaven praising God. Here he comes!! The King of Kings and Lord of Lords, riding on a white horse. Then the kings of the earth, along with the false prophets will be thrown into the lake of burning sulfur.

THE DAY THE FAT LADY SINGS

CHAPTER 20

The Thousand Years is described here where God will rule while the devil is bound up. Then he will be let out for a short time and then finally throw into the lake of sulfur where the beast and the false prophet had been thrown. After this, the Dead will be judged.

CHAPTERS 21 – 22

Behold a New Earth and New Heaven. Heaven on Earth is what it will be. The New Jerusalem. Read about it as it is described in this chapter and the next. Beautiful beyond what we can comprehend. JESUS is our light. No more sorrow, no more tears. We will be with him forever and ever.

So when does the fat lady sing ?

This is a good question, which has two (2) possible answers. But before we state the two answers, I think we have to elaborate on what we have learned up to this point. Let's go back to our chart and fill in a few more blanks:

THE DAY THE FAT LADY SINGS

EVENT	Matthew 24	Mark 13	Luke 21	Revelation
	Verses, in order of occurrence			SEAL # (VERSE))
Deceivers claiming to be Him	4	5	8	
Wars and Rumors of Wars	6,7	7	9, 10	# 2 (6:3)
Famine	7	8	11	# 3, (6:5) # 4 (6: 7)
Earthquakes	7	8	11	
Persecution	9	9	12	# 5 (6:9)
Turning away from the Faith	10			
Betrayers & Haters	12	12	17	
Increase in Wickedness	12			
Gospel preached throughout the World	14			
Abomination	15	14	24	
Great Distress	21	19	24	
False Christ	23	21		
False Miracles	24	22		
Sun Darken	29	24	25	
Heavenly Bodies Fall	29	25	25	# 6 (6:12)
THE MISSING DETAILS OF THE GOSPELS				Chapters 7 through 13
Sign in the sky of the coming of the Son of God	30	26	27	
Angels will gather the elect (Rapture)	31	27	28	Chapter 14:14
Bowls of God's Wrath				Chapter 16
Coming of the Son of God				Chapter 19
Millennium				Chapter 20
New Heaven and Earth				Chapters 21 & 22

THE DAY THE FAT LADY SINGS

SO WHEN DOES THE FAT LADY SING ?

Let's examine the following order of events:

1. Deceivers will come
2. Wars and Famine will increase
3. Persecution will increase
4. Wickedness will increase
5. The Gospel will be preached throughout the World
6. The Abomination will occur
7. The first half of the Tribulation will occur
8. The second half (Jacob's Trouble) of the Tribulation will occur

9. The Rapture occurs: **Answer #1: The Fat Lady Sings for the Believers and they avoid the Wrath of God**

10. Then God's Bowls of Wrath begin
11. Jesus returns with the Believers for the Battle of Armageddon
12. Jesus wins the Battle (obviously)
13. Babylon falls

14. The Beast and Unbelievers are judged: **Answer #2: The Fat Lady Sings for the Unbelievers and they will suffer under the Wrath of God**

15. Then the Lord creates a NEW HEAVEN and NEW EARTH

THE DAY THE FAT LADY SINGS

THE ONLY QUESTION THAT REMAINS IS: WHERE DO YOU FIT IN??

I urge you to accept Jesus Christ as your own personal Lord and Savior today

MY DECISION
Believing that Jesus Christ died for my sins and that he rose again on the third day, and that he will come back again in the future, I now confess Him as my Lord and Savior.

Date _____

Name _____

Now Devote Yourself to Following Him and to the Daily Reading of The Holy Bible.

MARANATHA
Come, Lord Jesus, Come

THE DAY THE FAT LADY SINGS

SALVATION ROAD

We Are All Sinners and Can't Do Anything Worthy Of Salvation
Romans 3:23 - For all have sinned and fall short of the glory of God.

We All Deserve Eternal Punishment For Our Sins
Romans 6:23 - For the wages of sin is death (eternal death = Hell), but the gift of God is eternal life in Christ Jesus our Lord.

Jesus Loved Us And Died for Our Sins.
Romans 5:8 - But God demonstrates his own love for us in this: While we were still sinners, Christ died for us.

Salvation Is Not Earned, It's A Gift From God Through Faith
Ephesians 2:8-9 - For it is by grace you have been saved, through faith and this is not from yourselves, it is the Gift of God, not by works, so that no one can boast.

THE DAY THE FAT LADY SINGS

If You Accepted Jesus As Lord & Savior, Tell Someone

Romans 10:9 & 10 - If you declare with your mouth, "Jesus is Lord," and believe in your heart that God raised him from the dead, you will be saved. For it is with your heart that you believe and are justified, and it is with your mouth that you profess your faith and are saved.

Romans 10:13 - Everyone who calls on the name of the Lord will be saved.

THE DAY THE FAT LADY SINGS

ABOUT THE AUTHOR

"Papa Joe" De Clemente has been married to his wife, Janet, since August 1969 and he has 4 children and 11 grandkids. He is a retired Aerospace Electrical Engineer and a Contracts Manager.

Being raised in a religious home, he attended church regularly, however, he never committed his life to Jesus Christ until June 28th 1974, when he was 27 years old. Once a believer, the Lord led him and his wife to a good Bible Believing Church where he started to study the Holy Scriptures and Biblical Prophecy.

The Spirit of God completely changed his outlook on the Family, Life, Eternity and Faith in the Lord. Over the next several decades, Papa Joe served in the following ministries:

- Christian Service Brigade Leader
- Church Elder/Deacon
- Church Trustee
- Bible School Superintendent and Teacher for Adults and Kids
- Missionary Committee Leader
- Vacation Bible School
- Short Term Missions trips to Niagara and the Philippines
- Volunteer at a Boy's Christian Camp
- Christian Music Ministry
- Church Usher

Email Contact: PapaJoeD@Yahoo.Com

Made in the USA
Middletown, DE
08 August 2024

58773341R00027